The Heritage Collection

Pretty Yende
COURAGE TO SAY YES

Letitia deGraft Okyere

Illustrated by Roseen

Lion's Historian
PRESS
Amplifying Authentic Voices

The Heritage Collection for Young Readers

Pretty Yende: Courage to Say Yes

Copyright © 2025 by Letitia deGraft Okyere

Illustrator: Roseen

Layout designer: Nasim Malik Sarkar

Library of Congress Control Number: 2025918582

All rights reserved.

No part of this publication may be reproduced, stored in a retrieval system, a database, and/or published in any form or by any means, electronic, mechanical, photocopying, recording or otherwise, without the prior written permission of the publisher.

ISBN 978-1-956776-32-4 hardcover
ISBN 978-1-956776-33-1 ebook

Published by Lion's Historian Press
https://www.lionshistorian.net/

In loving memory of Thandi Rose
and to all the other women in "The Pretty Army" who have
made Pretty's journey in the world of opera possible.

> Every inch of my soul resonates when I sing because I think that is my gift. I can only give myself. And I thank God for the talent. And I thank God for the ears that listen.

Contents

Chapter 1: Born in Piet Retief 1
Chapter 2: First Music Lessons 3
Chapter 3: The Seed Takes Root 5
Chapter 4: A Change is Coming 7
Chapter 5: First Encounter with Opera 9
Chapter 6: What is this Sound? 11
Chapter 7: The Ndlela School Choir 13
Chapter 8: A Solo Soprano 15
Chapter 9: The Big Decision 17
Chapter 10: Preparing for Cape Town 19
Chapter 11: Training at UCT 21
Chapter 12: Training at Teatro alla Scala 25
Chapter 13: The Big Break 27
Chapter 14: A Star Emerges 29
Chapter 15: A Song for a King 31
Chapter 16: Her Roots 33
Epilogue: A Bright Future 35

Glossary 39
Roles Played 41
Timeline 43
Quiz 46
Match Role and Opera 47
References 48
Other Books in the Heritage Collection 50

CHAPTER 1

Born in Piet Retief

Pretty Yende was born on March 6, 1985, in Piet Retief, located in South Africa's province of Mpumalanga. Pretty is the oldest of four children to Petros and Thandi Rose Yende. Pretty and her siblings grew up in a happy home where her parents did their best to shield them from South Africa's harsh political climate. They were surrounded by a close-knit extended family and church community that helped to instill the tenets of the Christian faith.

Piet Retief, Pretty's birthplace, is a small town rich in Zulu traditions. Though known for timber production, choral music plays an important role in the lives of its residents. In fact, singing is a part of South Africa's culture with a chorus for every situation, joyful or sad, or for expressing seasons of victory or struggle. The Yende household was steeped in this custom because everyone had a melodious voice. In the evenings, whether the family gathered to prepare meals or relax after dinner, there was always singing. "Pretty Girl," as her mother called her, was a shy child, but singing, dancing, and hand clapping brought her out of her shell.

CHAPTER 2

First Music Lessons

Little Pretty spent a lot of time with her maternal and paternal grandmothers. In the Zulu culture, it is customary for firstborn children to have a special bond with their grandparents. Hence, Pretty was also "firstborn" to her grandmothers, and they treated her like a princess. Pretty's grandmothers shared all they knew with her and urged her to follow her dreams. Pretty had no idea what that meant, but she loved her grandmothers and soaked in all the advice she received.

Pretty's paternal grandmother, gogo KaDladla (Granny KaDladla) was passionate about music. On Sunday mornings, Pretty and gogo KaDladla walked six miles to church and back. As gogo KaDladla suffered from asthma, she took breaks during the journey, and the dusty road became five-year-old Pretty's music room. Sitting on a stone, gogo KaDladla brought out her hymn book and taught Pretty how to sing. The first hymn she learned was *Hlengiwe* (Redeemed) by Fanny J. Crosby. Each time Pretty got a tune correct, gogo KaDladla beamed with pride, and when Pretty staggered, she was full of encouragement. After gogo KaDladla got her strength back, she packed her hymn book back into her purse and the two continued their walk.

CHAPTER 3

The Seed Takes Root

At church, gogo KaDladla made Pretty share the hymn she had just learned with the congregation. At first, it made Pretty uncomfortable when gogo KaDladla put her on "stage" to sing. However, Pretty would sing because she hated to disappoint gogo KaDladla. Pretty did not want to make gogo KaDladla sad. Gogo KaDladla kept up with the lessons, and Pretty's vocal abilities grew. Pretty's music lessons from gogo KaDladla meant she joined in the family's evening songs with more confidence.

Soon, Pretty noticed that when she sang, the congregants at the Church of the Nazarene, where the whole family worshipped, enjoyed her singing. Pretty thought, if they love it, then I love it too! What made Pretty happy was the pleasure her talent brought to others. It was worth the challenge of overcoming her fear of taking center stage. Here, Pretty, the soloist, was born. Pretty's mother thought her daughter might have a future in gospel music; however, destiny had other plans. Grandmother was preparing Pretty for the global stage even though no one in the Yende household imagined that.

CHAPTER 4

A Change is Coming

Pretty completed her primary education and enrolled at Ndlela Secondary School. She still sang at church while also helping wherever the reverend minister needed her. The church discovered that Pretty was the one who sneaked onto the premises and cleaned the sanctuary to make it ready for the next service. At home, she cared for her younger siblings, two brothers and a sister, setting a good example. Pretty took her studies seriously, learning from her parents never to limit her future possibilities.

One evening after dinner, Pretty heard her father talk with her mother about buying a television for the living room. Her father thought that it would open the wider world to Pretty and her siblings, enabling them to learn about the heritage and cultures of the world. The radio only offered a limited choice of programs. In South Africa, the policy of apartheid or racial segregation had led to checks on television ownership. However, as democracy took hold, televisions became common. It was time for the Yende home to have one. Pretty's father had no idea that a television would make the critical link between Pretty's gift and a desired path for her future.

CHAPTER 5

First Encounter with Opera

When the television arrived, Pretty and her siblings were excited. Pretty knew her parents had made a sacrifice for the purchase, and she was grateful. Pretty looked forward to the evening when the family gathered to watch the news or a show. She did not mind that adults selected the program to be watched. At this time, South Africa was seven years into democratic rule with the second black president, Thabo Mbeki, in office, and television services had gone digital, giving viewers more choices.

One evening in 2001, Pretty was watching television with the family when an advertisement for British Airways played. The images were presented against the background of the "Flower Duet" in the opera *Lakmé* by French composer Léo Delibes. Suddenly, Pretty felt warmth filling her body as her eyes widened. She made an instant connection to the music; her heart had found what it yearned for, even though she had no idea it had yearned for it. Pretty's bond with the music went deep, and yet she had no understanding why. What is this music? What is this sound? Is this humanly possible? If so, could she create such a sound? Emotions on Pretty's face swung from quizzical to gleeful; her heart had discovered some possibilities. Pretty kissed her parents goodnight and went to bed.

CHAPTER 6

What is this Sound?

It was hopeless trying to sleep. Pretty's mind searched for answers to the questions flooding her imagination. At sixteen years of age, she could find none within herself. "I know what I will do," she thought. She planned to go to the music room to have a conversation with Mr. K.N. Sithole, the music teacher. Certainly, Mr. Sithole would know the answers to the multitude of questions she had. Pretty finally fell asleep, dreaming of the possibility of singing and giving others the same joy she got from the British Airways advertisement.

The next morning, Pretty was at school early, searching for Mr. Sithole. Even before Mr. Sithole was done with pleasantries, Pretty described the music from the advertisement. "What is that music?" she asked.

The teacher replied, "Opera." That was the first time she had heard that word. She wanted to know if the incredible sound was made by human voices. He laughed and patiently replied, "Yes."

"Then you must teach me, Mr. Sithole, if they can do it, then I can do it too." Mr. Sithole smiled at her enthusiasm. If gogo KaDladla successfully taught her traditional hymns, then she could learn this too.

"Well, Pretty, you have to join the school choir," he said.

CHAPTER 7

The Ndlela School Choir

Pretty joined the school choir. During practice, Mr. Sithole heard her singing and pulled her aside. "Do you think you can become an opera singer with a voice so small? Pretty, do you even know how to sing?" Mr. Sithole asked. Pretty knew she had to overcome her shyness; becoming an opera singer would require boldness. Pretty had to improve her skill.

At home, after finishing her homework and chores, Pretty found a quiet spot and turned on the radio, searching for classical music. She recorded musical pieces on cassettes and spent hours daily playing and singing over the music to develop her voice. During the next months, Mr. Sithole noticed an improvement in her voice and confidence. As Pretty's poise grew and her talent developed, she participated in competitions, singing with her school choir and community choirs like the Africa Sings Choir.

Pretty balanced her time between schoolwork, chores, and strengthening her voice. Pretty was taught by her parents not to be a victim of the political difficulties in the country. It did not matter that the school did not have a piano for lessons. Pretty and the other choir members learned to sing with a melodica. Pretty would soon become a choir leader both at school and church.

CHAPTER 8

A Solo Soprano

Years went by, and Pretty looked forward to her high school graduation. She was on the way to studying accountancy with a scholarship; she was good at mathematics. She would earn a good income because there were only few black accountants in South Africa. Pretty remained active in singing competitions and winning trophies. A table in her family's living room was decorated with shields, medals, and prizes, without room for any more awards. Pretty benefited not only from Mr. Sithole's coaching but also from the choral music community. She received support from the well-known South African choral music champion Ms. Nolufefe P. Mtshabe, and master of choir competitions, Mzwandile Matthews.

The South African choral eisteddfod for schools gave Pretty the opening to showcase her talent on a wider scale. In 2003, Pretty won the national schools competition. Pretty's performance of an aria by Mozart, "Batti, batti, o bel Masetto," placed her in the platinum category, leaving competition judges in awe of her gift, as had happened many times in the past. Pretty became recognized as a solo soprano after winning national championships. So now, what next? What would happen to her gift if she studied accounting?

CHAPTER 9

The Big Decision

The urge for Pretty to discard accounting became more difficult to ignore. Pretty yearned to discover the world of opera; since 2001, she had been unable to quench that fire. Pretty set her sights on the University of Cape Town's (UCT) South African College of Music (SACM). Her eisteddfod success and participation in a music program at the college, made possible by a prize she had won, would strengthen her application. Also, she had "The Pretty Army," those in her life – parents, family, church, community, voice coaches – who kept her grounded and focused on her pursuits.

Pretty appreciated that gogo KaDladla's objective went beyond voice lessons. Her grandmother helped her to overcome shyness to reveal her true self. Pretty knew that being able to share her gift without barriers would be essential for the operatic platform that she was ready to explore. Pretty's heart had found something magnificent, and she simply could not let it go.

With the decision made, Pretty had to share her big plans with her parents. They were first shocked by the news. No more accountancy? What? Opera singer? Could there be a future in that? Opera should be more of a hobby than a career. They worried that she might not find work after her training. However, the more they stared into Pretty's eyes, the more they recognized that their daughter's heart was set on this career. Petros and Thandi Rose gave their consent, having faith in Pretty's determination and her gift.

CHAPTER 10

Preparing for Cape Town

Pretty, driven by her faith in God and a desire to develop her gift got accepted to UCT with a scholarship for opera studies in 2003. Pretty had no idea what to expect at UCT. No one in her family had been to university. Pretty did not know about black international opera stars like Leontyne Price and Kathleen Battle. Thoughts of leaving home and moving to a big city made her nervous. When her father asked her if she had any doubts, to mask her uncertainty, she responded, "How do I conquer the world if I don't first train?" with laughter while her stomach churned with worry.

Despite all the unknowns she faced, Pretty would make one factor certain: her choice of voice coach. It would have to be none other than Prof. Virginia Davids, an award-winning international opera singer turned teacher. Pretty made a call to Virginia Davids, insisting that she become her student. This was not normal practice. Usually, this decision was made on campus with the instructor, but Pretty believed in the impossible made possible.

Pretty completed her final year at Ndlela High School, breaking glass ceilings as the first ever female top student. A few months later, her eyes blinded with tears, Pretty headed to Cape Town, 950 miles from Piet Retief.

CHAPTER 11

Training at UCT

Pretty was right to feel anxious because at UCT, there were a lot of new experiences. In the past, she sang to a single instrument; here, there were orchestras of fifty members with instruments she had never seen before. There were fanciful costumes and elaborate make-up, and students with amazing voices and talents. Pretty asked herself if she deserved to be at the SACM; after all, she had no formal classical training.

However, Pretty still believed in impossible dreams. She was a sponge, learning to perfect her gift. Prof. Davids, known as Mama V by her students, taught Pretty to appreciate her voice as well as the talent in others. The world has enough room for diverse gifts to shine. Under Mama V's wings, Pretty learned to draw audiences into her performances. Pretty also studied with Prof. Angelo Gobbato, the renowned director of opera. He encouraged her to go beyond the quest for a flawless performance to one that reaches the listener's soul for a more lasting impact. He told Pretty she had to become as fluent in Italian as she was in her native tongue, Zulu.

Pretty worked hard, graduating from UCT cum laude for both her undergraduate and postgraduate studies. Her performance at UCT demonstrated that she had a unique voice with the ability to capture the roles she played successfully. Pretty discovered that she loved acting and learning the different languages of opera, Italian, French, and German.

Pretty's parents could not be prouder, and her mother's joyful ululating resonated in the hall during her graduation ceremony.

Done with UCT, Pretty was at another crossroads. Her business-owner father and schoolteacher mother did not have the resources to send her abroad for further training. Pretty sought a step that would move her closer to her dream of becoming a professional opera singer.

> Find your purpose and learn how to serve the world in the best way you can, because that's what you were destined for.

CHAPTER 12

Training at Teatro alla Scala

Pretty got an idea. Participation in competitions would showcase her talents. Pretty registered for the first of many, embarking on what would become a winning spree. In 2008, for example, Pretty won two prizes at the 's-Hertogenbosch event in the Netherlands: a cash award and a role as Micaëla in Bizet's *Carmen* at the famous Riga Opera in Latvia in 2010.

Pretty went on to win first prizes at the Belvedere, Caballé, Bellini, and Savonlinna competitions. All these wins and others gave Pretty the exposure she needed, but it was the 2009 Belvedere competition that changed her life. Pretty won fifteen prizes, the first time one person won all categories, beating 158 finalists. She got a place on the Young Artist Program at the Teatro alla Scala (Theater at the Scala) Academy, known as La Scala, in Milan, Italy. It was a gift from Ilias Tzempetonidis, casting director at La Scala, who had served on the Belvedere jury.

For two years, Pretty studied with great Italian artists like Mariella Devia and Mirella Freni. Mirella Freni suggested that Pretty focus on the bel canto range of music, and it became Pretty's foundation for the roles she has played. When classes were difficult, Illias encouraged her to be content with the little successes that came her way. She never missed a rehearsal at the opera house. Pretty completed her studies in 2011, the first ever African to graduate from La Scala's Academy of Lyric Opera. Pretty ended that year with another first, winning all categories of the Operalia competition.

CHAPTER 13

The Big Break

Pretty, now a graduate of La Scala, waited for her big break. How long would the wait be? Her parents had taught her that it was one thing to dream, another to live the dream. Pretty returned to Teatro alla Scala in early 2012 to play the Priestess in *Aida* in her professional debut after graduation. There were other appearances that year, as Musetta in Puccini's *La bohème*, Norina in *Don Pasquale*, and a concert with Dionne Warwick and Andrea Bocelli, all in Italy.

Finally, in December, while on vacation with her family, Pretty's manager called. Would she be available to play Countess Adèle in Rossini's *Le comte Ory* at the New York Metropolitan Opera House, about four weeks away? Pretty would be replacing another artist who had fallen ill. She jumped at the opportunity even though she had never heard of the opera before. Due to travel issues, Pretty had a week to learn the part, in French, before her debut in January 2013.

Opening night arrived and the opera house, with over 3,500 seats, was full. A nervous Pretty thought, "What am I doing here? They really wanted someone else." Then, during the first scene, Pretty tripped on a stair, falling on her hands and knees. While the audience gasped, wondering if she would have the courage to return to the stage, Pretty found the cure for her bout of anxiety. She put her chest out and gave her best. She showed the depth of her gift by easily coping with the opera's high notes. The praise reviews Pretty received launched her career as an international opera singer, leading to calls from agents.

CHAPTER 14

A Star Emerges

Pretty repeated the role of Countess Adèle in Vienna after her success in New York. She returned to South Africa later for a collaboration with the Cape Town Opera, for her debut as the first black Lucia in Donizetti's *Lucia Di Lammermoor*, appearing with the Cape Town Philharmonic Orchestra. That same year, the President of South Africa, Jacob Zuma, presented her with the Order of Ikhamanga in Silver for achieving international recognition for her excellence in opera and for being an inspiration for young musicians.

Pretty went on to mount stages all over the world, from London's Royal Opera House to the Deutsche Oper Berlin, and from Gran Teatre del Liceu in Barcelona to the San Francisco Opera House. The roles she played included Rosina in the *Il barbiere di Siviglia* (The Barber of Seville), Susanna in *Le nozze di Figaro* (The Marriage of Figaro), Adina in *L'elisir d'amore* (The Elixir of Love), Violetta in *La traviata* (The Fallen Woman), and Pamina in *Die Zauberflote* (The Magic Flute). She sings at concerts and recitals. When she performs "I Feel Pretty" from *West Side Story*, her audience can't help but burst out laughing. Pretty is also a recording artist with two albums, *A Journey*, released in 2016, and *Dreams* in 2017. Unknown to Pretty, as she was making her way through these major milestones, she was heading toward a special opening, one that most artists can only dream of.

CHAPTER 15

A Song for a King

Pretty had a little secret! King Charles III, monarch of the United Kingdom, was planning his coronation. Everyone wondered who would be performing as the last coronation occurred seventy years ago. Pretty had that special invitation! The request came in December 2022 when Pretty was performing in Vienna. Pretty had met King Charles III earlier that year at the 75th anniversary of the Royal Philharmonic Orchestra held at Windsor Castle. Pretty gave two arias, which left the royal delighted by her talent.

The time grew closer for the May 2023 coronation, and Pretty got excited. Then, the unthinkable happened. Pretty, in Vienna again, injured her ankle days before the event, but she was not giving this honor up. Pretty was going to make it, even if she had to crawl her way there. Thankfully, when the time came for her journey to London, her ankle felt better.

The historic and exciting day arrived, and Pretty made her way to Westminster Abbey. Dressed in a beautiful yellow gown, Pretty flitted up the Abbey's stairs like a butterfly. She sang "Sacred Fire," specially composed by Sarah Class for King Charles III and Queen Camilla, breaking another glass ceiling, the first African artist to perform a solo at a British monarch's coronation. Pretty did not just sing to the new king and queen, but to the twenty billion people watching across the world. Pretty started her singing career in a church, and after ten years on the world's most famous opera stages, Pretty shared her gift with the largest audience at yet another church.

CHAPTER 16

Her Roots

Though Pretty has ascended to stardom, she has not forgotten her roots as a girl from Piet Retief in South Africa. In 2010, she appeared with other stars at the Cape Town City Hall for an *Excellence out of Africa* trust concert to support young South African artists. Three years later, Pretty was back home to launch the Pretty Yende Foundation (PYF); "giving one the opportunity to choose today for tomorrow." PYF focuses on developing musical potential in the young people of Piet Retief. Pretty performs concerts and operas in Cape Town to share her talent and inspire the younger generation.

Pretty takes advantage of every opportunity to give back, helping young students to learn about classical music and develop operatic talent. Pretty has performed in operas for school-age children to teach them how to enjoy classical musicals with a live orchestra. She was tickled during one meeting with students, she asked a little boy, "What is opera?" and he burst out "OOOooo" with an imitation of a tenor. Recently, Pretty returned to her old school to encourage others by sharing her journey. Pretty holds master classes, teaching young singers the art of opera. She has learned that dreams do come true, and if so, then she must help others realize their dreams too.

EPILOGUE

A Bright Future

Pretty's journey continues with the support of "The Pretty Army," a group of loved ones who provide encouragement as she explores open doors. Pretty never forgets the God who watches over her, the warmth of her family, and her roots in Piet Retief. Pretty has learned that it is possible to live your dream with dedication and resilience. When her quest for the world operatic stage commenced, all she had was faith that it was possible, a determination to enhance her gift, and a desire to bring joy to others.

Today, Pretty sings in Italian, French, and German. She was the first black woman to have sung Lucia di Lammermoor, in Cape Town, Berlin, and Paris. She was the first black woman to play Violetta in a production of *La traviata* tailor-made for her. As Maria, she infused Zulu in *La fille du régiment*. Pretty has played all four leading women – Olympia, Antonia, Giulietta, and Stella – in *Les contes d'Hoffmann*. Pretty often teams up with artist Nadine Sierra for concerts singing arias and duets. She has performed with world-famous singers like Andrea Bocelli and Renée Fleming at several events. Just a year ago, she was invited to perform at the reopening of the Notre Dame Cathedral in Paris, delivering an unforgettable version of "Amazing Grace."

Pretty is breaking barriers in an art form traditionally seen as only for whites and society's elites. Recognition for her work includes national honors from South Africa, Italy, and France. Pretty enjoys creating moments

of magic for her audience and works to make opera more attractive to the younger generation, as well as inspire black women to pursue their dreams in opera. This ambition started in her home, encouraging her younger sister Nombulelo, who is a winner of international competitions (e.g., 2018 Bellini, 2023 Operalia), to study classical music. Pretty's brothers, into contemporary music, look forward to a family collaboration.

Pretty's eagerness to live up to whatever possibilities exist drives her career, in much the same way as it demanded that Mr. Sithole teach her opera or Mama V take her on as a voice student. She makes her native country, South Africa, proud as she lives her dream of giving joy to others through her gift. With her Christian faith as her foundation, and the love and support from her family, Pretty is always ready to embrace avenues made available by "The Pretty Journey," grateful that her life has become an inspiration to others.

> Nothing is impossible. Don't let the world scare you away from your dream.

Glossary

Apartheid	Apartheid or racial segregation was enforced in South Africa from 1948 until the 1990s. It was imposed upon the non-white majority by the white minority.
Aria	An aria is a type of song commonly found in opera. Arias may be performed with a full orchestra or instruments.
Batti, batti, o bel Masetto	Translated *Beat, beat, handsome Masetto,* is an aria for sopranos in the opera *Don Giovanni*, composed by Wolfgang Amadeus Mozart.
Bel canto	Italian for "beautiful singing." It is a style of operatic singing that indicates a full and smooth vocal technique.
Eisteddfod	A Welsh term for competitive festivals for music and poetry. In South Africa, choral eisteddfod gives young South Africans the opportunity to participate in talent competitions in music, theater, dance, and fine arts. It is a platform for preparing students for careers in the performing arts.
Flower Duet	The "Flower Duet" is a duet that is sung in the first act of the opera *Lakmé*, composed by Clément Philibert Léo Delibes. It was first performed in Paris in 1883.
Mozart	Wolfgang Amadeus Mozart was born on January 27, 1756, in Salzburg, Austria. Mozart is recognized as one of the greatest

composers of Western-style music. His major works include *The Marriage of Figaro* and *The Magic Flute*. He died on December 5, 1791.

Mpumalanga	South Africa is divided into nine provinces for administrative purposes. Mpumalanga Province is in the east, sharing a border with Kwa-Zulu-Natal, Limpopo, Free State, and Gauteng provinces. The Kingdom of Eswatini (formerly Swaziland) and the Republic of Mozambique lie to the east. Mpumalanga's provincial capital city is Mbombela.
Opera	This is a drama or theatrical work with several parts or acts. It is set to music with singers and instruments. The staging includes dramatic costumes and scenery.
Teatro alla Scala	The Theater at the Scala is an opera house in Milan, Italy, opened in August 1778. It is recognized as one of the leading opera houses in the world. Its school, Accademia Teatro alla Scala (La Scala Theater Academy) provides professional training in all aspects of opera. The Young Artist Program is a two-year tuition-free program for performers.
Zulu	The Zulu nation is a branch of the Bantu ethnic group located in the KwaZulu-Natal province in South Africa. The Zulu make up the largest ethnic group in South Africa.

Roles Played

(Additional information: name of opera and composer.)

Adèle
Le comte Ory (Count Ory)
Gioachino Rossini

Adina
L'elisir d'amore (The Elixir of Love)
Gaetano Donizetti

Amina
La sonnambula (The Sleepwalker)
Vincenzo Bellini

Amira
Ciro in Babilonia (Cyrus in Babylon)
Gioachino Rossini

Berenice
L'occasione fa il ladro (Opportunity Makes a Thief)
Gioachino Rossini

Cleopatra
Giulio Cesare in Egitto (Julius Caesar in Egypt)
George Frideric Handel

Elvira
L'italiana in Algeri (The Italian Girl in Algiers)
Gioachino Rossini

Elvira
I puritani (The Puritans)
Vincenzo Bellini

Fiorilla
Il turco in Italia (The Turk in Italy)
Gioachino Rossini

Gilda
Rigoletto
Giuseppe Verdi

Ismene
Mitridate, re di Ponto (Mithridates, King of Pontus)
Wolfgang Amadeus Mozart

Juliette
Roméo et Juliette (Romeo and Juliet)
Charles Gounod

Leila
Les pêcheurs de perles (The Pearl Fishers)
Georges Bizet

Lucia
Lucia di Lammermoor
Gaetano Donizetti

Manon
Manon
Jules Massenet

Maria
La fille du régiment (The Daughter of the Regiment)
Gaetano Donizetti

Magda
La rondine (The Swallow)
Giacomo Puccini

Micaëla
Carmen
Georges Bizet

Musetta
La bohème (The Bohemian)
Giacomo Puccini

Norina
Don Pasquale
Gaetano Donizetti

Priestess
Aida
Giuseppe Verdi

Olympia, Antonia, Giulietta, and Stella
Les contes d'Hoffmann (The Tales of Hoffmann)
Jacques Offenbach

Pamina
Die Zauberflote (The Magic Flute)
Wolfgang Amadeus Mozart

Rosina
Il barbiere di Siviglia (The Barber of Seville)
Gioachino Rossini

Susanna
Le nozze di Figaro (The Marriage of Figaro)
Wolfgang Amadeus Mozart

Teresa
Benvenuto Cellini
Hector Berlioz

Violetta
La traviata (The Fallen Woman)
Giuseppe Verdi

Zerline
Fra Diavolo (Brother Devil)
Daniel Auber

Zoraide
Ricciardo e Zoraide (Ricciardo and Zoraide)
Gioachino Rossini

Timeline

Highlights of Pretty's Journey to International Stardom
Ndlela Secondary School, Piet Retief
South African College of Music, Cape Town

2008 — Two prizes, International Vocal Competition 's-Hertogenbosch (Netherlands)

2009 — First prize in each category (fifteen prizes), International Hans Gabor Belvedere Singing Competition (Austria); First prize, Montserrat Caballé International Singing Competition (Spain)

2010 — First prize, Vincenzo Bellini International Competition (Italy); First prize (shared), International Singing Competition of Savonlinna Opera Festival (Finland); First prize, 6th Leyla Gencer Voice Competition (Turkey); Micaëla in Bizet's *Carmen*, Riga Opera (Latvia)

2011 — Graduate, Teatro alla Scala in Milan (Italy); First prize, Placido Domingo's Operalia competition (Russia)

2012	Arca D'Orco Prize young talent, Premio Internazionale Arca d'Oro (Italy)
2013	Countess Adèle in Rossini's *Le comte Ory*, New York Metropolitan Opera House (U.S.A.); Silver Order of Ikhamanga (South Africa); Mbokodo Award in Opera (South Africa)
2017	Best Recording Solo Recital Award *(A Journey)*, International Opera Awards; Newcomer of the Year Award, Echo Klassik (Germany); International Achiever Award, 23rd South African Music Awards (South Africa)
2018	Readers' Award, International Opera Awards; Cologne Opera Award (Kölner Opernpreis) (Germany)
2019	Knight of the Order of the Star of Italy (Ordine Stella d'Italia) (Italy)

2022	Office of the Arts and Letters, ceremonial badge of honor (France)
2023	Performance at the coronation of King Charles III and Queen Camilla (U.K.)
2024	Performance at the reopening of Notre Dame Cathedral (France); a star on the Johannesburg Theatre Entrance Walk of Fame (South Africa)
2025	Honorary member of the Royal Academy of Music (U.K.)

Quiz

1. Where was Pretty born?
    - (a) Piet Retief
    - (b) Cape Town
    - (c) Johannesburg
    - (d) Pretoria

2. Who gave Pretty her first music lessons?
    - (a) Mother Thandi
    - (b) Father Petros
    - (c) Sister Nombulelo
    - (d) gogo KaDladla

3. Who was Pretty's music teacher at Ndlela Secondary School?
    - (a) Angelo Gobbato
    - (b) Virginia Davids
    - (c) K.N. Sithole
    - (d) Nolufefe P. Mtshabe

4. Which role launched Pretty's career as an international professional opera singer?
    - (a) Rosina, *Il barbiere di Siviglia*
    - (b) Countess Adèle, *Le comte Ory*
    - (c) Violetta, *La traviata*
    - (d) Elvira, *I puritani*

Quiz Answers: ADCB

Match Role and Opera

	Role		Opera	
A	Fiorilla		*La fille du régiment* (The Daughter of the Regiment)	1
B	Amina		*La traviata* (The Fallen Woman)	2
C	Zerline		*Don Pasquale*	3
D	Magda		*La sonnambula* (The Sleepwalker)	4
E	Violetta		*La bohème* (The Bohemian)	5
F	Maria		*Fra Diavolo* (Brother Devil)	6
G	Musetta		*La rondine* (The Swallow)	7
H	Norina		*Il turco in Italia* (The Turk in Italy)	8

Match Role Answers: A8, B4, C6, D7, E2, F1, G5, H3

References

"Biography." Pretty Yende, 2025, https://prettyyende.com/. Accessed 1 March 2025.

Vokwana, Thembela. "The making of Pretty Yende." *IOL,* 2024, iol.co.za/ios/behindthenews/2023-05-13-the-making-of-pretty-yende/ The Conversation.

"In Conversation with Pretty Yende: Moderated by Elena Park." YouTube, uploaded by San Francisco Opera, 14 December 2022, https://www.youtube.com/watch?v=VbKTOgOQ6OU.

"In Song: Pretty Yende." YouTube, uploaded by San Francisco Opera, 4 November 2022, https://www.youtube.com/watch?v=yG5MujmmSnk.

Fairman, Richard. "Opera Singer Pretty Yende: 'I was touched by something almost supernatural." *Ft.com,* 30 December 2020, https://www.ft.com/content/5874c3ac-11d5-4935-bbae-dddc6524316c.

Salazar, Francisco. "The Butterfly – Pretty Yende's Never-Ending Search for Artistic Freedom." *Operawire*, 4 March 2017, operawire.com/the-butterfly-pretty-yendes-never-ending-search-for-artistic-freedom/.

Goldberg, Melissa. "Opera Star Pretty Yende's Surprising Journey to the Stage." *Oprah.com*, 16 May 2017, oprah.com/inspiration/opera-star-pretty-yende-interview-o-magazine-may-2017#ixzz4hJq5PCBG.

Huizenga, Tom. "Pretty Yende, 'A Journey'." *NPR.org*, 8 September 2016, https://www.npr.org/2016/09/08/492855308/pretty-yende-a-journey.

"Pretty Yende: An Opera Star Whose Rise Began With A Fall." *Deceptive Cadence NPR*, 20 March 2015, https://www.npr.org/sections/deceptivecadence/2015/03/20/393879727/pretty-yende-an-opera-star-whose-rise-began-with-a-fall.

"Flying high with opera singer Pretty Yende and British Airways." YouTube, uploaded by British Airways, 23 February 2015, https://www.youtube.com/watch?v=KXiecFIod9E&t=135s.

Haw, Penny. "South African Opera Export Extraordinaire, Pretty Yende: A Profile." *Penny Haw,* 30 December 2014, pennyhaw.com/2014/12/30/south-african-opera-export-extraordinaire-pretty-yende-a-profile/.

"Pretty Yende performs in her hometown, Piet Retief." YouTube, uploaded by sabc3topbilling, 24 July 2014, https://www.youtube.com/watch?v=m_m-_BYFKXU.

da Fonseca-Wollheim, Corinna. "Little Time to Prepare; Now a Legacy to Keep." *New York Times*, 1 Feb 2013, https://www.nytimes.com/2013/02/02/arts/music/little-time-to-prepare-now-a-legacy-to-keep.html.

Cotton, Pia. "One Small Stumble, One Giant Leap." *Wall Street Journal Online*, 2013, https://www.proquest.com/blogs-podcasts-websites/one-small-stumble-giant. Accessed 4 April 2025.

Other Books in the Heritage Collection

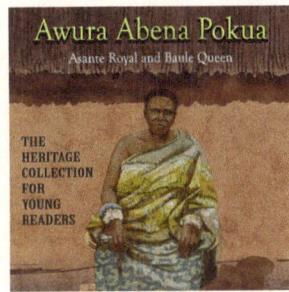
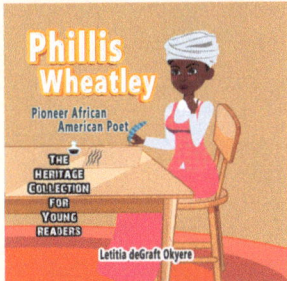

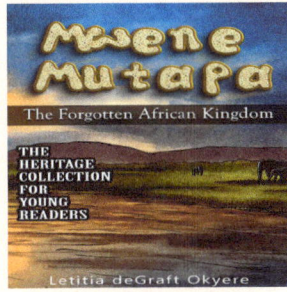

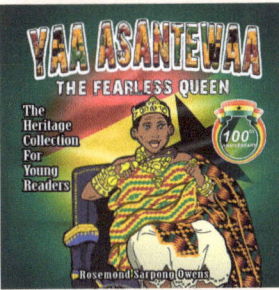
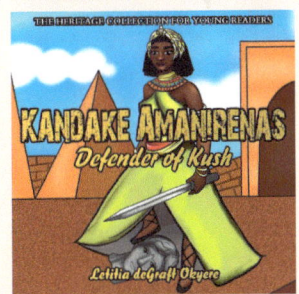
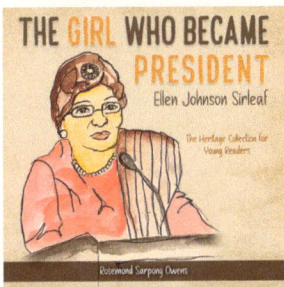

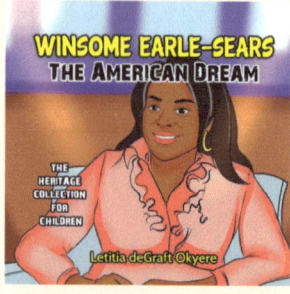

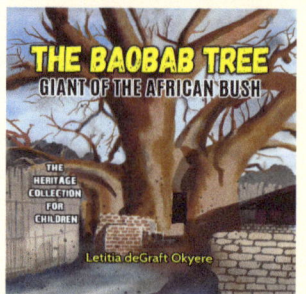

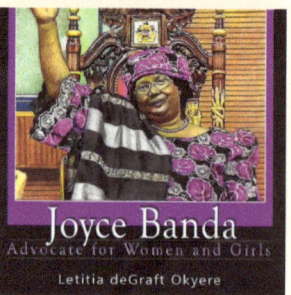
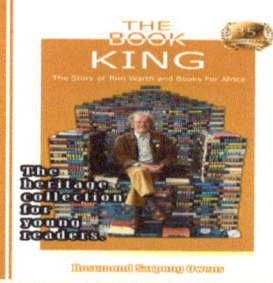

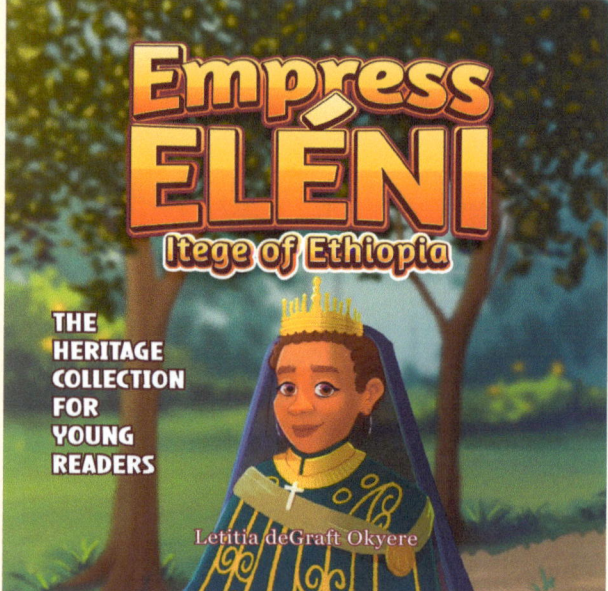
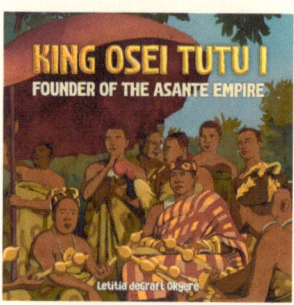

www.ingramcontent.com/pod-product-compliance
Lightning Source LLC
Chambersburg PA
CBHW041407010526
44107CB00015B/1100